THE STORY OF A RIVER

HUDSON

ROBERT BARON & THOMAS LOCKER

FULCRUM PUBLISHING

GOLDEN, COLORADO

Dedicated to the memory of Marietta Baron

Library of Congress Cataloging-in-Publication Data

Baron, Robert C.
Hudson : the story of a river / Robert Baron and Thomas Locker.
p. cm.
Summary: Presents an imaginary journey back in time to the birth of the
Hudson River and examines its history, pollution and clean-up, nearby
Native American and European settlements, and the river's appeal as a
tourist destination and literary subject.
Includes bibliographical references.
ISBN 1-55591-512-4 (hardcover)
1. Hudson River (N.Y. and N.J.)—History—Juvenile literature. 2.
Hudson River (N.Y. and N.J.)—Environmental conditions—Juvenile
literature. [1. Hudson River (N.Y. and N.J.)—History. 2. Hudson River
Valley (N.Y. and N.J.)—History.] I. Locker, Thomas, 1937- II. Title.
F127.H8B37 2004
974.7'3—dc22
2003022331

Design by Nancy Duncan-Cashman
Printed in China
0 9 8 7 6 5 4 3 2 1

Fulcrum Publishing
16100 Table Mountain Parkway, Suite 300 Golden, Colorado 80403
(800) 992-2908 (303) 277-1623
www.fulcrum-books.com

AUTHOR'S NOTES

This is the story of the Hudson River, one of America's earliest settled rivers
and the gateway to the American West. It also relates to the story of any
river: the Mississippi, the Colorado, the Thames, the Nile, or the Rhine.

~

People need fresh water in order to live. And for centuries, people
have lived by the rivers of the world and used them for drinking,
for food, for transportation. We have also used the rivers as dumps,
putting trash and hazardous materials into the rivers and oceans.
When we poison the rivers, we poison ourselves. The earth needs
our assistance to correct the mistakes we have made in the past.

~

Modern people stand in awe of the achievement of scientific thinking.
It has created an amazing body of knowledge and, through technical
innovation, has diminished much of the toil of existence. But
writers such as Rachel Carson have recognized a dark side
from the use of science—chemicals that threaten biodiversity,
industrial inroads into our fragile environment, growing
populations, and the capacity of modern civilization to destroy the planet.
The belief that we are separate from nature and our desire to control
nature appears to be leading us in the wrong direction. Perhaps
it is time to consider the possibility of other ways of thinking.

~

It is our hope that *Hudson: The Story of a River* will inspire the young to find ways
to encounter rivers with reverence and to live in harmony with them.

We are all part of nature and nature is part of us.

Storm King Mountain is one of the oldest rocks in the world.
A billion years ago, this granite mass rose up from deep in the earth.
It was shaped by cycles of ice ages and tropical seas.

The river that flows by the mountain was born when ocean tides
cut a channel and met a freshwater torrent from melting glaciers.
Today the Hudson River originates when a small pond in the
mountains of northern New York, Lake Tear of the Clouds, fills
and overflows, heading south 315 miles through a beautiful valley
flanked by ancient mountains. At the mouth of the river, salt water
from the Atlantic Ocean enters the Hudson, creating an extensive
estuary and forming unique wetlands habitats.

If mountains could speak, Storm King could tell *The Story of a River*.

Use your imagination and we will share this story.

Storm King's story began long ago. After millions of years,
soil formed on Storm King, and plants and animals appeared.
Ten thousand years ago, at the end of the last ice age,
Native American people moved up the Hudson River Valley.
They developed a way of living in harmony with nature, and for
thousands of years they inhabited an unchanging wilderness.

Geese, swans, ducks, herons, and other birds flew over the river
while more than two hundred varieties of fish, both salt- and
freshwater, used the Hudson River for spawning and feeding.

Four hundred years ago, Captain Henry Hudson sailed a Dutch ship,
the *Half Moon*, past Storm King Mountain and the vast wilderness.
The sailors watched eagles and osprey fly above waters
teaming with life. The ideas that subsequent settlers brought from
Europe of exploiting these natural resources began to rapidly
transform the Hudson River and its surrounding landscape.

The *Half Moon* sailed up the river that Native Americans
called the Mahicanitewk, the river that flows two ways,
due to the push and pull of the salty ocean tides.

Passing the ancient Catskill Mountains looming up in the
west, the crew observed that the river water, fed by streams
and creeks, grew clearer as the salt content diminished.
Realizing that the river had an inland source, they
abandoned their search for a Northwest Passage to China.

The crew observed Mahican villages carved into the forest
near the banks of the river. While Native Americans remained part of
the Hudson Valley until the late eighteenth century, they had no
immunity to contagious European diseases such as smallpox.
Those who survived were driven west by the expansion of the
colonial population and by the loss of traditional hunting grounds.

The mountain and the river saw it all.

First Dutch and German then English settlers took possession of the Hudson River Valley. They arrived with certain ideas and practices: European agricultural methods, notions of aristocratic land ownership and private property, the institution of slavery, and political ideas of liberty and equality.

Quickly they transformed the valley, cutting down the wilderness to create farms, building permanent towns, and creating roads that led to the river. The Hudson River Valley became a garden of prosperous farms. Boats carried farm produce to markets and taxes to the king of England.

But soon cries of "no taxation without representation," spurred by powerful ideas of liberty and democracy rang through the land. The Declaration of Independence was signed and the Revolutionary War began.

The English generals decided that the Hudson River was key
to their strategy to defeat the rebellion. They believed that
if they controlled the Hudson they could cut off the New England
colonies from the mid-Atlantic and southern colonies.
British forces, under General John Burgoyne, marched
south from Canada, and English ships sailed north.
One of the key turning points of the war, the British surrender
at Saratoga, occurred near the northern part of the river.

A constitution for the new republic was established based upon the
ideas of liberty and equality. But only men of property enjoyed
full equality and liberty; women, the poor, and people of color
were barred from political participation.

The first years of the new republic were a time of enormous energy and profound transformation. Using the ample waterpower of the streams and rivers, men built mills to create all types of products.

Ships from ports along the Hudson sailed around the world distributing natural resources and manufactured goods. Iron foundaries using charcoal from the forest and ore from the hills, produced cannons and armaments for military use. Although agriculture was the dominant activity, textile mills, factories, icehouses, and brickyards provided work for the floods of immigrants who came to America in search of a better life.

The mountain and the river saw it all.

Some people saw the natural world as more than a storehouse of commodities. America's first writers, called the Knickerbockers, used the wilderness of the Hudson River Valley as the setting for their novels and the subject of their poetry. Washington Irving, James Fenimore Cooper, and William Cullen Bryant wrote about our relationship with nature. Their work inspired tourists to travel upriver to witness the beauty of nature.

Many travelers stayed in mountaintop hotels and worshipped nature in the outdoor church of wilderness. In this untouched handiwork of the divine designer, they experienced God in nature.

We are all part of nature and nature is part of us.

Wealthy and powerful businessmen built mansions that
rivaled the castles of the Rhine on high places along the river.
As the population grew and industries continued to affect the
landscape, the forests dwindled. Art collectors requested images
of the vanishing wilderness.

America's first unique school of painting developed from a reverence
for the wilderness that industry and agriculture were destroying.
These Hudson River School painters, including Thomas Cole,
Asher Durand, and Frederic Church, used nature as a vehicle to see
a vision of God. They believed that people could respond to nature
and, by looking at paintings of the beauty of the natural world, could
improve their souls.

Rapid development of the valley transformed the Hudson River into America's commercial Main Street and New York City into America's major port. Bridges were built over and tunnels were dug under the river. An underground aqueduct just north of Storm King carried Catskill water to a thirsty New York City. Canals were cut connecting the Hudson with the coal fields of Pennsylvania and the waters of Lake Champlain. The Erie Canal in 1820 linked the Hudson River to the Great Lakes and became the gateway to the West for thousands of travelers.

Steamboats went up and down the river and railroads were built alongside it, cutting off the wetlands that helped clean the water. Fishermen, who for generations had relied on the river for their livelihood, could no longer catch enough fish. The Hudson River was described as an open sewer.

Yet we are all part of nature and nature is part of us.

BILLINGS COUNTY PUBLIC SCHOOL
Box 307
Medora, North Dakota 58645

The idea of nature as a resource for commerce came into conflict with the painters' and writers' views that nature was a source of inspiration. When a power company decided to blast a hole in Storm King Mountain to build a hydroelectric power plant, citizens banded together to stop the irreversible destruction. Fishermen, historical preservationists, conservationists, and others joined in a coalition and filed a class-action suit to stop the power company. They argued that once the mountain was destroyed, it could not be restored. The striped bass that spawned at the base of the mountain would disappear.

An important and beautiful natural monument, a part of America's natural heritage, would be lost. Beauty, the power company's opponents argued, belongs to everyone. After seventeen years of legal and political debates, the courts ruled in favor of the coalition. This landmark ruling provided a legal basis for the environmental movement.

The mountain and the river saw it all.

American society continued its march toward greater equality.
Women obtained the vote, and people of color became protected
by civil rights legislation. Eventually the concept of rights began
to extend beyond people to the rest of the natural world.

New legislation, such as the Endangered Species Act and the
National Environmental Protection Act, safeguarded nature
against the excesses of human population and industry.
Some people view the clean air and water legislation as a
recognition that animals and plants, as well as the world
that sustains them, possess basic rights.

Armed with these new legal tools, an environmental movement
began actively pursuing and bringing to justice polluters.
In search of more profitable and less regulated locations,
many of the heavy industries left the Hudson River Valley.
Some went south, some went west, and others left the country.
They left behind a river contaminated with oil spills, pesticides,
raw sewage, toxic chemical compounds, lead, and mercury.
Cleaning up and containing the pollutants is a continuing process.

After decades of abuse by private industries and individuals
that used the river as a dumping ground to dispose of waste,
the tide turned. Rachel Carson and other writers sounded the
alarm that humans were destroying the life-sustaining natural world.

Numerous individuals and private organizations joined the fight
to stamp out pollution at its source. A replica of a Hudson River Dutch
sloop called the *Clearwater* was built and sails up and down
the river, educating people about the importance of clean water
and air. The river is still polluted; people cannot drink the water,
eat the fish, or swim in many locations. Nonetheless, every year the
river grows cleaner. Eagles, almost completely wiped out from
the Hudson River Valley, once again soar above the water.

We are all part of nature and nature is part of us.

Now try to imagine a day in the future when you take
your children to see a beautiful river. Perhaps you can
help them to think like a mountain about time and a river.

We are part of nature and nature is part of us, but just part.

What makes human beings special is the ability to think and act.
The world will be better when all of us come to realize the
fragility of our earth and act in support of nature, respecting
the rights of all other parts of the living planet.

We know that when we change nature, we change ourselves.
Everything is connected to everything else. We have the
means to preserve life on earth if we have the will.

Many parts of nature are beyond the control of humankind. In the warmth of sunlight, clouds form and bring the gift of fresh water to the lakes and to the river, bringing life to all who live in or near it.

We now see ourselves as a part of nature and of planet earth, a speck of dust in a solar system in the galaxy of the Milky Way, traveling in a vast universe of stars. Looking inward at the tiny parts of the atom or outward to the edge of the universe, each discovery leads to yet another mystery, to a recognition of the splendor and glory of it all.

Human beings have lived for many years by the edge of the Hudson River and have spent endless hours studying its beauty. We must be part of the story of the river. With words, images, or music, we can praise the glory of creation and work to preserve it for future generations.

The mountain and the river are watching.

*S*ome books to read about the Hudson River and its history:

In this series:
John Muir: America's Naturalist   Thomas Locker
Rachel Carson: Preserving a Sense of Wonder   Joseph Bruchac and Thomas Locker
Walking with Henry: Based on the Life and Work of
    Henry David Thoreau   Thomas Locker

Additional reading:
American Sublime: Landscape and Scenery of
    the Lower Hudson Valley   Raymond O'Brien
The Catskills: From Wilderness to Woodstock   Alf Evers
Chronicles of the Hudson   Roland Van Zandt
Civilizing the Machine: Technology and
    Republican Values in America 1776–1900   John Kasson
A History of New York   Washington Irving
The Hudson   Carl Carmer
The Hudson: From the Wilderness to the Sea   Benson J. Lossing
The Hudson River Highlands   Frances Dunwell
The Hudson River School:
    American Landscape Artists   Bert Yaeger
The Hudson Valley and the American Revolution   New York State Education Department
John Burroughs' America: Selections from the
    Writings of the Hudson River Naturalist   Farida Wiley, editor
The Life and Works of Thomas Cole   Louis Legrand Noble
The Natural Paradise:
    Painting in America 1800–1950   Kynaston McShine, editor
Nature and the American   Hans Huth
North Country: An Anthology of Contemporary
    Writings from the Adirondacks and the   Joseph Bruchac, Jean Rikhoff,
    Upper Hudson Valley   and Alice W. Gilborn, editors

Painters of Faith   Gene Veith
The Spy: A Tale of the Neutral Ground   James Fenimore Cooper
Thanatopsis   William Cullen Bryant